Are You Ready to Recharge Your Battery?

Secrets of Work/Life Balance

Are You Ready to Recharge Your Battery?

Secrets of Work/Life Balance

Sharon M. Weinstein

Are You Ready to Recharge Your Battery?

Secrets of work/life balance by Sharon M. Weinstein

Copyright ©2019 by SMWGroup Publishers

Cover Design and Graphics by Kimb Williams
Printed in the United States of America

ISBN-13: 978-0-9989384-1-7

Available from Amazon.com and other online stores
For information about this title or to order additional copies, including customized copies, contact the publisher: SMWGroup, LLC or at: https://smwgroupllc.com, 1.202.798.0092, info@smwgroupllc.com

iv

Advance Praise...

"**Are you Ready** to face the need for work/life balance and take action? Sharon's newest release is a must-read for everyone, at every stage of life."

Mindi Vogel, Employee Benefits Advisor
The Megro Benefits Company

"**Are You Ready**? spoke directly to me and opened the door to the recharging process. Sharon Weinstein takes you to the core of readiness, offering great tips, techniques, and solutions."

Heather Taylor, CEO
After a Loss

"I read this at just the right time. I love work and pour myself into it, but I see the downside. Sharon provides a thought-provoking approach to achieving the balance I crave."

Colleen Marzilli, Assistant Professor
University of Texas at Tyler

"An IRONMAN™ competitor, and life-long athlete, I am continually challenging myself to try new approaches. As a communications expert, I easily related to the value of Sharon's book, **Are You Ready**. She communicates and demonstrates the steps you need to begin your work/life balance journey."

Lisa Copeland, CSP
Ironman Competitor

"I have been very fortunate to work for a great family business that understands the need for work/life balance, fully realizing that a happy employee is a productive employee. Isn't that what we all want? In **Are You Ready**, Sharon provides insight and direction for introspection with tools and techniques for adjusting your prospective and career prospects."

Mark Drury, VP, Business Development
Shapiro & Duncan

"In **Are You Ready**, Sharon addresses the challenges of work/life balance, and the opportunities for action. This is a must-read for anyone who wants to more effectively deal with this widespread topic."

Bob Dabic, Master Chair & Best Practice Chair
Vistage

"Are you struggling with work/life balance? Got more to do than time to do it? Sharon's tips will ease your stress and help you regain control of that to-do list. Take her advice to heart; I encourage you to read this book!"

Pat Iyer, Author
52 Writing Tips: Fast Ways to Polish Your Writing
patiyer.com

"Once again, Sharon leads by example and is sharing tips and techniques for living a more satisfying life in **Are you Ready**. If greater work/life balance is on your radar, this book is for you!"

Nancy Trick, WW Clinical Market Manager
Becton Dickinson

"**Are you Ready** addresses the challenges of work/life balance, and the opportunities for action. This is a must-read for everyone, everywhere."

Jeffrey Tredwell, DPM, Chairman

DAPSHealth

Dedication

I get my charge each day from my family and my work. I find joy in the journey, appreciate my contributions, express gratitude and kindness, and value a life in balance!

Are You Ready to Recharge Your Battery? Secrets to work/life balance is dedicated to my husband, Steve, our kids and their incredible families.

- Sharon

Preface

If you are busy with a demanding job and family and friends who seek your time and attention, you are blessed, but only if you can handle it. Consider the stressors in your own life, including the things that deplete your energy and bring you down.

You may be a workaholic like I was; I thought the day was thirty hours long. I tried to fit a schedule into each of those hours to achieve life to the fullest. My strategy did not work.

As one who has reinvented myself professionally throughout my career, I am aware of the challenges of work/life balance. I worked long hours and I always felt as if something was missing…and that something was family time. Balancing a career or business with your personal life can be challenging, but it's not impossible. *Are You Ready to Recharge Your Battery* offers actions you can take to build the life and career you want, need, and deserve.

"To keep a lamp burning, we have to keep putting oil in it."
- Mother Teresa

We need to recharge our batteries—so get set, get ready, and let's go! We'll explore the process of engaging in life and work, prepare for a change and a charge, manage time and resources, and reinvent ourselves. The process begins here and now, with content and action steps at the end of each section that empower you to act, recover, and restore a full charge!

Where will you be in six months if you don't start now?

Table of Contents

PART ONE

Engaging in Life and Work

With 65 percent of U.S. employees citing work as a significant source of **stress** and more than one-third reporting chronic work **stress**, workplace **stress** can affect both individual well-being and organizational performance, according to the American Psychological Association Center for Organizational Excellence. We want to engage in life and in work, but sometimes life gets in the way. In Part One, we address the reality of stress and our role in engaging and managing human resources or human lives.

Chapter One

Back to Reality and
Back to Stress

SOUND FAMILIAR?

What are your three greatest stress triggers? After a few relaxing days off, are you eager to get back to your job, or anxious because of that job? Think about it! You've had a great vacation, or even a great weekend. Now, it's time to get back to reality—to whatever stressed you in the first place and necessitated that important respite. There is so much to do and no time to get it done. The first few days are hectic until you settle back into your routine. Emails and snail mail remain unanswered. Your voicemail box is full. What you thought would be an easy transition has become a life challenge, and you wonder how you will get through each day with your mind intact.

Life can be challenging and stressful. Creating work/life balance is critical to success and survival. Living the dream, and overcoming the pain is something else.

In today's economy, stress may be attributed as much to *having* a job as to *not* having one. Layoffs around the country impact workers in all settings. If you fear the loss of your job—even a job you don't like—you experience stress. How will you feed your family? How will you pay your bills? Will you have to think twice before making routine purchases? We all have different stress triggers, but work tops the list.

Causes of work-related stress include being unhappy in your job, a heavy workload, long hours, unclear expectations of your work, bullying and toxic work settings. Is that what you want to return to? Vacations and holidays come and go, but stress is ongoing. This is reality!

"Reality is the leading cause of stress among those in touch with it."

- Lily Tomlin

How will you cope?

Apply these simple strategies for finding life balance, and begin to deal with the challenges you would otherwise face:

Are You Ready to Recharge Your Battery?

- Create realistic goals.
- Manage your time wisely.
- Eat healthy.
- Learn when to say no and when to let go!

Minimize the pain by choosing one to two strategies to tackle; this process will put you on-track—starting now!

Chapter Two

Is It Really Teamwork?

Have you ever increased your workload, failed to meet commitments, lost sleep, and put yourself—or someone else—at risk? I have done all of these!

Stress in the workplace

Longer hours, greater workloads, staff reductions: These and other factors contribute to stress in the workplace. For those who work shifts, stress is a constant. It affects fatigue, safety, retention, and outcomes. Shift work disorder (SWD) is a circadian rhythm disorder. About 20% of the U.S. workforce is involved in rotating shifts; their schedules are in direct conflict with the body's normal rhythm. They experience difficulty adjusting to the ever-changing sleep-wake schedule. The consequences are extreme: increased accidents, more sick leave, irritability, and mistakes.

Not saying no, assuming responsibility for more hours/shifts: These and other factors contribute to increased workload, greater stress levels, and the potential for errors.

You are a team!

Think of yourself as a team. At the helm is *you*. "You" can be viewed as a team of "personalities" or "sub-people," each of which has different needs and styles. Some are impulsive. Others are doubtful. Some represent strengths and talents.

Your team has needs:

1. The physical "you" needs nutrition, exercise, and rest.
2. The emotional "you" needs forgiveness, love and compassion, laughter, self-actualization, and joy.
3. The mental "you" needs self-supportive attitudes, positive thoughts, and self-image.
4. The spiritual "you" needs inner calmness, openness to creativity, and trust.

How do you function without the entire team on board? When your needs are met, you are better able to deal with stress. Perhaps the word "no" does not come easily to you. Perhaps your boss requires you to work extra hours or extra shifts; can you say "no?" Is now the time to say "no" to greater workloads, and "yes" to greater safety and outcomes?

Chapter Three

Are You Engaged—
Without the Bling?

When you think of superior customer service, what name comes to mind? For me, it is Nordstrom! Nordstrom has a reputation of going the extra mile for you, the consumer! The Nordstrom story has become a classic example of service at its finest.

Why? Because Nordstrom employees take ownership; they become a part of the process; they deliver on the expectations of management and they feel great about being there!

But we cannot all work at Nordstrom—nor would we want to. We hear about "consumer experience" more than ever, but whether you work in retail, travel, hospitality, or healthcare, you cannot deliver a great consumer or client experience without great employee engagement.

And engagement starts at the top.

Are staff in your organization treated as well as those they serve? Engaged employees are:

- Energized
- Committed
- Action-oriented
- Problem-solvers
- Critical thinkers
- Innovators

Engaged employees have a voice, and their voices drive change within the organization. They see, touch, and feel engagement every day. Engagement is woven within the vision, mission, and goals of the institution, and the staff knows it.

Companies that sustain, connect, and communicate engagement in their ranks create something larger than the sum of their parts—an engaged workplace.

Employee engagement is: Getting up in the morning thinking, "Great, I'm going to work. I know what I'm going to do today. I've got some fantastic ideas about how to do my job well. I'm looking forward to seeing the team and helping them accomplish something meaningful today."

Though employee engagement and job satisfaction are closely related, engagement is about performance, not satisfaction. The last thing you want is a team of satisfied-but-underperforming employees.

What Can You Do?

Boost performance by making it easy for employees to own their tasks and focus on results. Make that process fun.

1. Give staff a voice by listening with intention and respecting their input.
2. Understand drivers of engagement, such as purpose, influence, and value.
3. Offer meaningful recognition through employee recognition programs, paid time off, and celebrating employee successes.
4. Extend opportunities for personal and professional growth with continuing education, staff development, and mentoring programs.

By following these steps, today's employers put the "E" in Engagement—just like Nordstrom.

"The past, the present, and the future are really one; they are today."

- Harriet Beecher Stowe

Chapter Four

Human Resources or Human Lives?

Do you want to be valued as a product or as a human being? Chances are you have thought about this concept during an especially frustrating day at work or after a long sequence of stressful experiences. Why does it matter? It matters because today, more than ever before, employees are feeling undervalued, insecure, less recognized, and overwhelmed. Employees are stressed, and at the core of this stress is the work environment. Within many industries, we have mastered the importance of a healing environment. How much attention do we give to lighting, lack of clutter, better views, privacy, HVAC, healthy plants, and art? Can the work environment be supportive and human-centered? Can it be less overwhelming?

Overwhelmed Employees

The concepts of work/life balance have been lost, thanks to a proliferation of technology and the breakdown in barriers between work and life. When your work life and personal life blend together under the guise of "multi-tasking," both suffer. The sheer complexity of our lives creates internal distress and can wreak havoc on our bodies. And, we do it in the name of being the "loyal employee," also known as "human capital." It has become so intense that the focus on human capital management (HCM) has intensified.

Human Capital Management: the new HR

HCM perceives people as assets whose current value can be measured, and whose future value can be enhanced through investment. Have you given much thought to investing in your people, because according to master people manager, Sam Walton, "The way management treats associates is exactly how the associates will treat the customers?"

Think about HCM as a responsibility for attracting, developing, and managing the firm's biggest asset—people. Are you managing human capital/resources or human lives in your organization? An organization that supports HCM provides employees with clearly defined and consistently communicated performance expectations.

Managers are responsible for rating, rewarding, and holding employees accountable for achieving specific business goals, creating innovation, and supporting improvement. An organization that supports and manages human lives puts its people first and creates an experience for them.

Managing Lives

What about the relationship between employers and employees? How are we defining and managing those relationships? How do we view the dedicated employee? If we follow the Sam Walton model, we know that how we treat the employee is how the employee will treat the customer or client. For years, in marketing programs across the country, we studied our internal and external customers. We knew that we had to add value to our internal customers if we wanted to succeed.

How can we manage what matters most?

Are you adding value to the lives of those with whom you work? Are your employees dedicated to your mission and vision?

Consider these steps:

1. Value your staff.
2. Involve staff in strategic planning.
3. Become a manager of lives, rather than resources.

"Whoever is happy will make others happy too."

- Anne Frank

It's no longer

a secret!

ACT now...

- Declutter your space.
- Avoid distractions at work.
- Engage with others.
- Follow the two-minute rule.

But, what's next? You've committed to engaging in life and in work. Yet, life still gets in the way. Could you be suffering from burnout? Are you ready for a change and a charge?

PART TWO

Burning Out and Ready for a Change and Charge

Are you ready to address the need for change? In Part Two, we face fatigue, self-care, a much-needed digital detox, and making your environment your choice. Let's deal with burning out and facilitating change.

Chapter Five

A Troubling Question: Who Owns Fatigue?

Are you fatigued? Do you feel as if you cannot work for another minute without falling apart at the seams? We talk about fatigue, but whose responsibility is it? Who owns fatigue?

We all do! We are all stakeholders in the fatigue management process, and we all own it!

The employer...

...can do much to shift the paradigm and create a culture of safety, wellness, and caring. Clear and compelling visions start us along a path of generating a future we deserve to have. Regardless of the business entity, everyone assumes responsibility for fatigue management and good outcomes.

Contributing factors might include:

1. Changes in leadership.
2. Decision dilemma.

3. Inability to find/retain top talent.
4. Fewer resources.
5. Greater expectations.

Any employee...

...is responsible for practicing healthy behaviors that reduce the risk of working while fatigued or sleepy, resulting in arriving to work alert and well rested, and promoting a safe commute to and from work. This responsibility might require that you to reject a work assignment that compromises the availability of sufficient time for sleep and recovery from work—for example, when your shift ends at midnight, and you are expected to return to work, fully rested, by 7:00 a.m. We all have different recovery times. Our bodies and minds are unique, and this concept often involves scheduled shifts and mandatory or voluntary overtime. We need to listen to our bodies; we know them best. It is everyone's responsibility to address one's own, as well as co-workers', fatigue. Employees must be responsible and know their limits. Is it even possible to repair the system. If yes, how do we repair the system?

Are You Ready to Recharge Your Battery?

The system predicts the outcome; start the repair process now, by:

1. Ensuring positive outcomes for staff and clients.
2. Instituting fatigue management protocols.
3. Scheduling staff wisely.

"The body says what words cannot."

\- Martha Graham

Chapter Six

Mastering Self-Care

Are you working harder than ever before? Many of us are working harder than we ever imagined. Our hours and days are longer. Our free time is nominal. We may have fallen into the technology trap because it is available 24/7. Examine your own situation and be honest with yourself. What is in your way? Is it you? You can tip the scales in your favor with the addition of counterbalancing techniques like time management, prioritization, health awareness, and openness.

Remember the flight attendant's instruction to "Put your own oxygen mask on first?" Well, it's true. We can't do for others if we're exhausted and burned out.

Practice saying "No"

Boundaries are an important form of self-care. They help you protect your time and energy, so it's spent on what's most important to you. Check-in with yourself and listen to what's right for you and act accordingly. There is nothing wrong with considering your own needs.

Everybody knows someone who has asked, and to whom we just cannot say, **No**. Trust me, *"No is a complete sentence."* It does not require justification, excuses, reasons, or supporting documentation. It is simply a **No**.

It's okay to say, "NO!" Like you, I probably said, "Yes" much too often. I worked the extra hours. I took home the assignment that was due the next day. I stayed late to help my peers. I went out at 11pm to Walmart in search of a lunchbox for a visiting grandchild. I returned the books to the library, completed the website revisions, led the project team, and…I was known as the "finisher." My former boss often referred to me in that way to describe the fact that I left nothing undone, and I could be counted on to get the job done…no matter what it might take in terms of time, money, energy, and spirit.

And what did I get in return? I had great satisfaction in the fact that my work was complete, required little change, was timely, and that I could be counted on. I loved that feeling, and I loved helping others. But, one day I realized that I could no longer work 100-hour weeks, and that I could no longer be the only one on a project team completing the project. I realized that I had no time for myself, for my family, and for the life that I wanted to live. It was time for a change!

Regrets

Now, I regret the times when I failed to say "no" just because of peer pressure. Let's learn to face the music here: saying "yes" to everyone is stressful. It's selfish. And it's not good for your mental, physical, and spiritual health! My friend, it's time you start saying "no." "No" to people you don't like, "no" to parties and events you don't want to attend, and certainly "no" to activities that don't make you a better person.

How does one escape a trap that one has built?

Go ahead and say "no," because:

1. You don't owe anybody anything.
2. You can never control everybody's opinion of you.
3. You're the only one who can really identify your priorities in life.
4. Life moves on.

"Everyone thinks of changing the world, but no one thinks of changing himself."

- Leo Tolstoy

Chapter Seven

Digital Detox Time

Do your devices make your life easier or more challenging? Have you ever just wanted to be device-free? You have a plethora of "smart" devices and apps that facilitate your life's work, keep you on track and on time, turn on the lights and TV, and shut them down. Wouldn't it be great if you had an app or device that allowed you to master self-care the smart way?

As a business owner, employee, consultant or student, you work long hours and probably take little time for yourself. The time is now to get "smart," and start by forming a digital detox (yes from those amazing devices and apps that you cannot live without).

The power of five

Try these five easy steps to regain your time and energy, while getting "smart" about self-care:

1. Think about the communication tools you use and select one! Then, request your clients to use that tool to communicate with you.
2. Set parameters for time online; you do it for your kids, and you should do it for yourself.
3. Schedule breaks for yourself; even 15 minutes per day will make a huge difference in how you feel and your performance.
4. Add mindfulness to your routine while walking and eating.
5. Make a gratitude list; think about people, places, and things that bring you joy.

What's smart about "smart" devices and apps?

These devices do not ensure smart use of your time. It's time to get "smart" by:

1. Identifying those things that must be done and those that can wait.
2. Listing the groups to which you must belong.
3. Completing your work and take a break!

Are You Ready to Recharge Your Battery?

Even though there is so much to do and so little time, take time for yourself and make being "smart" and in balance a part of your daily routine! You will thank yourself, and those around you will thank you too.

"In your thirst for knowledge, be sure not to drown in all the information."

- Anthony J. D'Angelo

Chapter Eight

Your Environment, Your Choice

Your environment is your space…it is your body, and the settings in which you live, work, and play. Your body probably started out on an even playing field 25 or more years ago. And, your home and work settings have influenced your body's ability to adapt—to thrive and survive today and forever. Think about where you live, work, and play, and think about the sources of stress that are present on an almost daily basis and influence your ability to be well and to stay well.

Let's begin with choice!

The choices that you make about what you put into your body and that with which you surround yourself, impact your outcomes—how well you feel, how productive you are, and how good you look. Are the choices that you are making healthy, or will they impair function? For example, is there a can of soda on your desktop—eager to turn your body into an acidic environment that will slow you down, swell you up, and put you to sleep? I hope not!

The work/life connection

A crisis exists today. Millions of people are unwell, suffering from the stressors that are part of modern living: lack of sleep, poor nutrition, exposure to dangerous pollutants, little or no exercise, and time pressures. And people—millions of people—are looking for solutions.

Workplace wellness programs are among necessities within the environment. Model programs for disease management are decreasing days lost from work, enhancing lifestyle, and increasing performance. As workweeks are expanding and stress levels are rising, more hours are spent at the workplace, and health takes a toll.

We all have the same requisite number of hours in a day—only 24. And yet, we try to extend those hours and make them equal 36 or more. It is virtually impossible, and our productivity demonstrates our failure to adhere to the workday as normal.

A workplace is only as good as how it treats its workers.

Today's employers are constantly seeking ways to assist their workers in managing their job responsibilities and their personal obligations and needs. Strategies for work/life balance help create supportive, healthy work environments, strengthen employee commitment and loyalty, and result in more productive workplaces and improved customer satisfaction.

As professionals, we have expectations from our work environment, from those with whom we work, and our future. Oprah Winfrey suggests that, "Right now you are one choice away from a new beginning—one that leads you toward becoming the fullest human being you can be."

If your path is paved with good intentions, but your work is unrewarding, and your time is not your own...negotiate. Think things over and make a change.

What can you do now?

1. Negotiate for change in the workplace.

2. Work with your employer to improve the environment, your outcomes, and the company's success.

3. Be an advocate for yourself.

"When people go to work, they shouldn't have to leave their hearts at home."

- Betty Bender

It's no longer

a secret!

ACT now...

- Track your time.
- Make an appointment (with yourself).
- Say no to internet addiction.
- Create a dedicated "homework" space at home.

You've burned. You've changed, and you need more! Are you ready to manage your time and resources to get to balance once and for all?

PART THREE

Managing Time and Resources

Do you often wonder how others seem to do it all? In Part Three, we get to the heart of the matter, discover our spine, focus ourselves, and identify the need for a personal recharge.

Chapter Nine

Too Much to Do and Too Little Time

Are you doing more or less than you did a year ago? Would you like to know how to achieve more by doing less? Do these questions come to mind?

Are you kidding me?

Is this even possible?

How can I make it happen?

When do I start?

Is Balance Possible?

Work/life or workday balance...what is it, and why does it matter? Whose responsibility is it? It is ours—we all share the responsibility of implementing strategies to ensure work/life balance.

Annual conferences, regional meetings...they spell long days, long weeks, and the need to be "on" all the time with multiple responsibilities pulling you in multiple directions!

There is so much to do and so little time! How can you achieve more and do less?

Is all this a cliché or is it reality? In today's environment, it certainly seems that it is indeed our reality—a reality of the times in which we live and our expansive scope of work. Balancing work and personal life can be a challenging task. Are you prepared for the challenge?

It's your turn and time

Is your performance impaired because you are out of balance? Are you caught up in the balancing act, unable to do it all and care only for others in your life without caring for yourself? You are only as good as you are balanced! If you do not take the time for yourself—yes, even with the array of responsibilities pressuring you now—you will not be the best that you can be. That personal best includes you as parent, partner, friend, professional, educator, student, or manager. That personal best is what will enable you to reach new heights in your career, to achieve your goals and to maintain your health.

It will result in great outcomes, allowing you to achieve more and do less, minus the stress.

Where do you find time?

Again, we each have only 24 hours in a day; maximize your time by:

1. Scheduling appointments for and with yourself.
2. Managing productivity, people, and resources.
3. Considering what matters most and put that first.

"We need to maintain a proper balance in our life by allocating the time we have. There are occasions where saying no is the best time management practice there is."

- Catherine Pulsife

Chapter Ten

Do You Have a Spine?

Have you been accused of not having a spine because you did not stand up for yourself or your beliefs?

A spine. You need one to survive and thrive!

"A lot of people are afraid to tell the truth, to say no. That's where toughness comes into play. Toughness is not being a bully. It's having backbone."

- Robert Kiyosaki

Have you ever felt used, abused, taken advantage of, insecure? Chances are, we have all felt that way at one time or another, especially in childhood. I grew up with very little—if any—self-esteem, and yes, I was walked on—and over—many times. I gravitated to folks similar to me. One of my first boyfriends was a wonderful guy who would give you the shirt off his back and never ask for a thing in return. And everyone took advantage of his generosity and kind spirit.

Are you too good to be true?

Being known as Mr. Good Guy may work for a while, but it certainly cannot last forever. At some point, even the most generous of us will finally say, "Enough!" Chances are, when that does happen, things have come to more than enough, and we are at our wits' end trying to decide how to get on with our lives and assert ourselves.

How much of a spine do you have?

To answer that question and determine where you stand and what you need to do to get out of your own way, ponder these questions.

1. Is the whole world out to get you?
2. Do you moan and groan?
3. Do you worry too much about what other people think?
4. Are you easily distracted from your goals?
5. Do you avoid all risks, even small ones?
6. Do you control what you will do each day, or do others control you and your behaviors?

How do you cope?

If your responses are anything like mine were at one time, it may be a good time to grow that spine, get a life, and move on! There's no time better than now!

1. Take a stand.
2. Say no when needed.
3. Ask for help.

"To succeed in life, you need three things: a wishbone, a backbone, and a funny bone."

- Reba McEntire

Chapter Eleven

Focus and Why It Matters

"The biggest adventure you can ever take is to live the life of your dreams."

- Oprah Winfrey

Have you ever put your keys away and forgotten where they are? Our chaotic lives can easily distract us from our focus. How many times in a day do you find yourself in a room, knowing you were there for a reason, but unable to remember the reason you went there? Or, at the end of the day with a heavy sigh, looking over your to-do list from that morning, you realize you barely made a dent in your list? We joke and attribute it to old age—even the young do this—but more likely it is a difficulty in maintaining focus.

Focus is what keeps us on track.

It's what we do when we have a goal to achieve. We keep focused on doing what we need to do to accomplish the tasks that cumulatively make up the goal. Focus is also an ability to remain undistracted. It is what we use to intently pursue a goal like running the Boston Marathon, studying for exams, writing a paper, or creating artwork. It is this kind of focus that is the source of the "Aha" moment we hope for when seeking solutions and setting goals. Getting to it—to that "Aha" moment of achievement or recognition—includes the knowledge of how to define your path and work your plan. Forbes Magazine published an informal study on "Aha" moments; this is my favorite: "No one—not your mother, your clients, nor the vendors you're working with—wants to tell you 'No' when you ask for something; most people want to find a way to tell you 'Yes.' My "Aha" moment was when I realized this and started asking for what I wanted in life."

Are you focused on what you want and need?

I truly believe in asking for what you want in life. That became reality when I proposed to my husband on our 5th date and we were married on the 10th day after we had met. What closed the deal for me? The very first phone call, which lasted 3 hours, in which he described his amazing family. Although he was an only child, and his dad had passed when he (my husband) was just 14, he depicted a family of which I wanted to be a part. And so, I asked by simply focusing and stating, "I'm not working on Wednesday, would you like to get married?" The rest is history!

Are you focused on what tomorrow may bring?

Try these simple tips:

1. Keep your eye on the ball.
2. Make decisions.
3. Prioritize.

Chapter Twelve

Downtime—Should You Recharge Now?

Your phone dies; you plug it in and recharge it! Your computer slows down; you delete extra backups, restore, and more!

Your body fails you, and what do you do? Can you change the batteries, recharge it, or take it in for assessment and repairs?

The Signal

Perhaps this is a signal, and it is time for a "creative pause" or disengagement. Our need for belonging is cited in Maslow's hierarchy of needs. Think of how it would feel to stop belonging for a few minutes of your time, to forget your "followers" for 30 to 60 minutes, or to stop "liking" every post that you see, merely because it is indicative of belonging.

Downtime is a good thing!

When was the last time that you took "downtime" or that much-needed break?" If and when you did, did you feel guilty for your lack of productivity?

What was the impact on your work, your relationships, your health? Did you find joy in the moment, and the satisfaction that comes from doing something for yourself? Did you take criticism from your colleagues, your family, your friends? Did you openly take that coveted downtime, or sneak a peek between heavy work schedules? How did that make you feel?

We can push our bodies and our minds just so far before they will fail us. The time has never been better for that well-deserved downtime!

Are you ready to commit to downtime? Have you wondered how to begin?

What can you do now?

Start with these easy steps:

1. Smile and smell the roses.
2. Enjoy the fresh air.

3. Unplug from the system that is wasting your personal batteries.

"At least once a week, I try to have one day where I have nothing planned so I can get up and just go back to bed and lay around and recharge my batteries."

- Dolph Lundgren

It's no longer
a secret!
ACT now...

- Turn your To-Do list into a Must-Do list.
- Do only what brings you joy.
- Keep the main thing the main thing.
- Deep breathe, meditate, hydrate (try an app).

But where are the answers? You've accepted my advice. This may be the time to reinvent yourself!

PART FOUR

Reinventing Yourself—The Balanced Way

Are you ready to reinvent yourself? In Part Four, we cover the simple life and possibilities—negotiating for balance, readiness, and the art of reinvention. It is time to recreate your future.

Chapter Thirteen

You Know That It's Possible—The Simple Life

How simple was your life when you were growing up, and how complex is it now? Think back about the days when life was indeed simpler!

"Finding a way to live the simple life is one of life's supreme complications."

- T. S. Eliot

Are you on overdrive?

Well, are you? Each of us, at one time or another, has felt overwhelmed. We hesitate to take a holiday, because when we return, the paperwork will be piled sky-high. We hesitate to attend a professional development program, because when we return, our development will be stifled by the amount of work that has been generated during our absence.

61

Now that I no longer work 100 hours per week, my life seems simple. In reality, life is not that simple—is it because of the plethora of material things in our lives?

Think back to your childhood. My dad was a contractor, so we had lots of bathrooms in our home, and even with five kids sharing bedrooms, we did not have to share a bath. My best friend's family consisted of a mom and dad, plus two teenage girls. They had a four-bedroom home with only one bathroom, and there were constant battles to see who got to use the bathroom first. If someone had a date or required additional prep time, the coveted bathroom could be inaccessible.

In my home, we lacked closet space, and most hanging space seemed to come from freestanding dressers with closet rods. When I think of how our own kids have grown up—with private rooms most of the time, luxury kitchens, wonderful yards, a phone in every room and more—I wonder how we existed. When our daughters ask me how we managed without a mobile phone, I smile and think back to the days of dial phones and party lines. Fast forward and think of your own kids and how much "stuff" they have! Think about how complex their lives are. Would they benefit from simplicity? Do they need T.S. Eliot to help them find the simple life?

A Personal Choice

Simplifying one's life is a personal choice as well as a process. To start, examine all areas of your life and determine at least five that can be simplified. For example, in the housing market crunch, my home was for sale for more than one year. That meant that each and every day, the beds had to be made, the dishwasher emptied, the laundry put away, the countertops clean. That meant fresh flowers in the kitchen and bathrooms and a decluttered environment. How does someone juggling multiple tasks declutter an environment—clear a desk in a home-based office? It is difficult...yet possible.

As a nursing student in a diploma school, we were often short-staffed. There may have been 40 patients on a ward with only a registered nurse, a student, and an aide. We all know that medications and treatments take priority, and we adjusted our time accordingly. If there was insufficient time for a full bath, we gave sponge baths or washed face, hands and bottoms. After all, no one ever died of dirt—they died of not having treatments done or not getting their medications. We simplified, and while we may not have been proud of the process, the outcomes were good.

How to implement the power of five

So, think of five things in your own life, and then begin your process!

1. Eat simpler foods but eat as a family.
2. Drop membership on a committee to free your time.
3. Clear out the clutter in your life to make it easier to find things.
4. Put things in their place.
5. Turn off the TV and spend TV time with the family.

Chapter Fourteen

Negotiating for Balance

Are you tired, overworked, emotionally and physically drained? Are your aging parents challenged, or is your young child ill? Is your partner out of work, or overworked? If any of these scenarios describe you, you may need balance. If you know your skills, abilities, and performance record are strong and valued, you have a solid footing for negotiating flexible work arrangements.

What is negotiation?

Practically, it's making the other person an offer or proposal that they may find more attractive than the next best alternative. Some consider negotiation to be the art of making deals. It is certainly that, but it also involves educating the other party about merits of your offer or proposal, or talents, skills, and actual or potential contributions. Negotiation is a key component of creating workplace balance and thus avoiding burnout.

65

What's your plan?

To negotiate successfully, you must do some advance planning. The process is simple, but each step is critical to the outcome. Remember that people never plan to fail; they do fail to plan.

1. Be prepared. Follow the tips and understand the rationale; know what you want and understand what the other party wants.
2. Open with your case; this demonstrates confidence. Then, listen actively.
3. Support your case with facts.
4. Explore areas of agreement and disagreement and seek understanding and possibilities.
5. Indicate your readiness to work together.
6. Know your options.

Work

Work is an ongoing negotiation — regardless of the work setting and your position within the organization. We just addressed the stressors associated with the workplace.

Examples might include staff negotiations related to hours, compensation, benefits, bonus targets and payouts, outcomes, expectations, performance, or co-workers. It might involve revenue-generation, cost-cutting or margin-optimization, customer/ client service issues or service recovery/customer service). Anything and everything involves the art of negotiation.

How can negotiation help?

1. Focus on mutual interests.
2. Offer a variety of ways to resolve issues.
3. Aim for an objective that benefits both parties.

"All great acts are ruled by intention. What you mean is what you get."

- Brenna Yovanoff

Chapter Fifteen

Are You Ready to Live and Work Stress-Free?

Are you the founder of your business, the CEO, the partner, or the boss? Are you the manager of your home, the parent, the caregiver? Founders, CEOs, bosses, managers, parents, caregivers—they are not always the best at taking care of themselves.

Taking Care of Business and Yourself

Whether you work for yourself or someone else, you show up, take care of business, and perhaps forget that the greatest commodity in your business is you; do you take care of you? If that answer is "no," or "not enough," you are ripe for stress.

Do you have a "Job" or a "Career?" A job is not the same as a career. Do you want a promotion or a paycheck; what are you willing to do to get it?

From my experience working at multiple professional companies over many years, I realized that there are two specific groups of working people. There are the people for whom career success and growth is most important and valued. On the opposite end of the spectrum, are working people who keep working at a job that offers both security and work/life balance. You may fall somewhere in between these two groups.

I Live to Work (Career First)

Who: People that focus on career growth at the cost of a healthy work/life balance might say:

- "I don't mind staying at the office late and checking email while on vacation to succeed."
- "I prefer to be rewarded by earning more money rather than having more vacation days."
- "I seek promotions at work in order to gain more responsibility and challenges."

I Work to Live (Balance First)

Who: People who keep the same job to maintain a predictable work/life balance often say:

- "I hate putting in overtime hours when it means less time for myself and my family."

- "I prefer a routine job over one that is more demanding."
- "I look forward to earning more vacation days as I advance in my career."

Which camp do you fall into? Are you like those people who wish to put balance first but feel trapped in a career achievement cycle? Do you put your career ahead of your goals because of the financial rewards and professional recognition? Do you know which camp best describes you?

Have you reached the point where you enjoy your career but want to get off the work-work treadmill?

Ask yourself these questions...

1. Does your own situation afford you the opportunity to maintain a stable job?
2. Can work/life integration help you achieve a sense of balance?
3. Are you committed to making balance a priority?

Think about the cost of stress...

It's time to consider the cost factors associated with stress. Could you possibly assign a dollar value to these:

1. Family
2. Health
3. Productivity
4. Relationships
5. Finances
6. Work

"A positive attitude turns 'I can't, and I won't,' into 'I have, and I will.'"

- Mandy Hale

Chapter Sixteen

Scary, Isn't It—The Idea of Reinventing Yourself?

"Just remember, when you're over the hill, you begin to pick up speed."

- Charles Schulz

Why are you here today? Are you over the hill like Charles Schultz, picking up speed, or growing wiser and more careful like Hemingway? Have you been in your present position for a year, two years, or more? Are you in a dead-end position that seems to lack a future? Do you hate your boss, or are you the boss?

Is it time for you to reinvent yourself?

I have done it several times. Growing up with parents who told me to learn to type because I would never amount to anything, I was challenged at an early age to be the best of the best. As the middle of five kids, I did not have "Middle

Child Syndrome," but I did have "Caught in the Middle Syndrome." And, it was not fun! So, I started at an early age to identify ways in which I could better myself, learn and do more, achieve great heights, and then start all over again.

As a nurse, I often worked hard, putting in extra hours and carrying an extra load. I was a good student...although an impatient one. I was always in anticipation of the next step...the next part of the obstacle course...the next challenge. As I think back, I realize that part of my wish to reinvent myself stemmed from a lack of self-esteem and an awareness that others were brighter, kinder, and that they came from what seemed to be (at least on the outside) loving families. So, I needed a new look, a new role, a new career—an opportunity to shine beyond my wildest dreams. And, I worked hard at it.

People reinvent themselves for different reasons. For some, it's the sudden realization that they're not happy or fulfilled. This is what's commonly called a "mid-life crisis." The reinventors, on the other hand, prefer the term "finding themselves," particularly when they're not in the mood to admit that they're flat out bored and need a change. Some of you may have kids who are still finding themselves; you may be that inner child yourself.

Some of my colleagues have chosen "preferment." Preferment is the ability to select those with whom you want to work and the projects you'd like to complete.

How about you—do you want to change, or do you have to change? Are you willing to challenge yourself to get what you want? Are you ready for a better version of you?

Think of your own reinvention and what it might look like. Narrow your wish list down to the top three reinvention choices; they will be fluid and subject to change.

1. Act towards them and watch what happens.
2. Reinvention is about a decision, a commitment, and action steps in support of that decision.
3. Make the decision yours and yours alone!

"Not knowing when the dawn will come, I open every door."
- Emily Dickinson

It's no longer
a secret!
ACT now…

- Simplify by five.
- Negotiate days off.
- Set your boundaries.
- Reinvent yourself.

Some say that everything is possible; not everything is probable. You've done the work and balance is well within your reach! When you rise up and when you lie down, reflect on the balancing act you've created and the next steps on your journey!

Are you ready to recharge your battery? These tools will jumpstart the process:

ENGAGEMENT

Awareness:	Note your presence in the moment.
Participate:	Play with a child and like a child; have fun.
Interactions:	Form relationships and enhance existing relationships.
Learn:	Learning is fun and enlightening.

ENVIRONMENT

Support:	Capture senior level support.
Choose initiatives:	Consistent with risk appraisals and claims history.
Model healthy behaviors:	Walk the walk and talk the talk.
Monitor:	Outcomes and impact on the organization.
Options:	Keep your options open to new ideas, people, places, and things.

MINDFULNESS

Morning:	Be aware of the smells, sensations, and sounds of morning.
Walking:	Focus on your breathing; experience the movement.
Interactions:	Think about what the other person is saying; experience verbal and nonverbal cues.
Be mindful:	Use an app as needed.

BALANCE SOCIAL MEDIA

Connectivity:	Take a self-imposed break at dinner and after 7pm.
Be verbal:	There is more to life than texting; return or place a call.
Create a plan:	For how you will connect and with whom.
Monitor:	Outcomes and impact on the organization.
Environment:	Keep devices out of the bedroom, bathroom and sacred spaces.

Summary

"Laugh and the world laughs with you; snore and you sleep alone."

- Anthony Burgess

Adding a smile and a laugh to life's challenges—the secret to a life in balance.

As the author of *B is for Balance, a guide to creating balance in life and at work*, and as one who has lived it, I know the importance of laughter...the best medicine. With today's hectic pace, we need a few moments of daily laughter; the more the better.

It is free of charge and readily available. What can laughter do? Laughter is good for you and your health. It relaxes the entire body, boosts the immune system, triggers the release of endorphins, and protects the heart! Laughter makes you feel good, relaxes you, and relieves tension. Are you starting to realize the impact that a smile, a little joy, and a good laugh can have in your own life?

As a diploma graduate from Pennsylvania Hospital School of Nursing, Philadelphia, I continued my education in Florida and Texas as I moved around the country and across the globe—somewhat of a pioneer at the time. No, I was not in the military, although that might have been a great choice. Rather, my husband (a successful hospital Chief Executive) and I took turns relocating for one another—always advancing within our careers. During this time, I also had three children...and they became expert networkers as they navigated within school systems and new neighborhoods. To some, this might appear stressful. To us, it represented a journey, an opportunity to meet new people, make new friends, and to exercise humor in the process.

Our journeys enabled us to own 16 homes in multiple states and an apartment in Moscow. Our journeys allowed us to look on the bright side of moving about—clean closets, constant purging, lack of clutter and the development of incredible organizational skills. Despite this constant activity—or perhaps because of it—our adult children are incredibly well-adjusted, outgoing, and yes, they do see laughter as the best medicine.

So, what about laughter? For years, our children referred to me as "50 Percent," meaning that 50 percent of the time (or less), I had a good sense of humor. I actually "got" a joke; I could laugh at myself. I think that I have now graduated to 90 percent. Sometimes, I am the first to see the humor in a situation or to come up with a great line. Of course, family members are still amazed! Sometimes, I get "it"—whatever "it" might be! And, my level of awareness has increased as I have transitioned within my career from a focus on intervention to one of health promotion and disease prevention.

Laughter has a place within every aspect of one's life. Laughter has enabled me to change my mindset, shift my paradigms and it has enhanced my well-being! Humor allows us to deal with stress more effectively; humor impacts healing and recovery time. And, humor has enabled me to grow personally and professionally.

As I have transitioned within my career, a sense of humor has helped. In my work with foreign Ministers of Health, Education, and Finance, I always needed to see the big picture of what was possible, but perhaps not always probable. In my consulting practice, I have integrated humor in my work with a focus on what "can be," rather than what "is." In my speaking career, I've learned the fine art of storytelling, with humor.

So, like me, step back, look at the big picture and use that perspective to help people feel good about themselves; that is the critical skill that's allowed me to touch the lives of people like you and me on a global scale! From personal experience, I know that sometimes it all comes down to the environment in which we live and work. That environment can hinder our ability to be well and can be a source of stress.

We can push our bodies and our minds just so far before they will fail us. The time has never been better to smile, to smell the roses, enjoy the fresh air, and unplug from the system that is wasting those personal batteries!

Alas, the secret is out of the bag!

Charge your battery now!

About the Author

An entrepreneur, author, and speaker, Sharon Weinstein is known as the "Stressbuster." She helps others prioritize never-ending "must do" lists into manageable goals to avoid burnout from seemingly ceaseless work. Her book, *B is for Balance, 2nd edition, 12 Steps Toward a More Balanced Life at Home and at Work*, was awarded First Place in Consumer Health by the American Nurses Association in 2015.

Prior to committing to balance, she directed the Office of International Affairs for Premier, Inc. and founded the International Nursing Leadership Institute (INLI). Sharon was a U.S. advisor to The Kremlin Hospital (yes, that one), creating a new healthcare infrastructure. Working 100 hours and three countries per week until she missed a family event after a four-day delay in Eastern Europe, she knew she needed to shift her paradigm and take control of her life. She's a classic example of reinventing oneself.

Fast forward two decades during which she founded two

businesses and non-profits and became one of only three nurses worldwide with the coveted CSP/FAAN designation, and you'll see why she's uniquely qualified to help those in high-stress industries where stress is a constant. Her expertise in leadership development, stress/fatigue management and service excellence helps you to answer the difficult question, "What if…"

A recipient of the Frist Humanitarian Award (HCA), Sharon is Past President of The National Speakers Association-DC (NSA) and current Chair of NSA's Certification Committee. She lives and works stress-free, sharing that BALANCE is not a fad, ad, or promotion. It is for everyone, every day.

Sharon's work has been featured in The Washington Post, The New York Times, USA Today, Speaker Magazine, Forbes, CEO Magazine, The Toronto Globe and Mail, The Chicago Tribune, and Nursing Management.

What you need to know:

In 2019, Sharon launched WOWTcomes™ to add much-needed WOW to programs, meetings, and processes!

Are You Ready to Recharge Your Battery?

WOWTcomes™ is your solution to providing WOW and great outcomes for the healthcare, hospitality and human capital industries and more!

WOWTcomes™ changes your value statement from ordinary to extraordinary. WOWTcomes™ is more than a program or service: it's an experience. Are you ready to experience a WOWTcome™?

Let her show you how!

More Books by Sharon M. Weinstein

Go for It...Mastering Negotiations

B is for balance...the road to stress management

B is for Balance, 2nd edition, 12 steps toward a more balanced life at home and at work

B is for Balance, a nurse's guide for enjoying life at work and at home

Plumer's Principles and Practice of Infusion Therapy, 9th edition with Mary Hagle

Plumer's Principles and Practice of Infusion Therapy, 4th, 5th, 6th, 7th, and 8th editions

Nursing without Borders...values, wisdom, success markers with Ann Marie T. Brooks

The Nurses Handbook of Intravenous Medications

Memory Bank for IVs

Restructuring the Workload: Methods and Models to Address the Nursing Shortage

Chapters...

Pharmacology, in Crudi, C. and Larkin, M., Core Curriculum for Infusion Nursing

Developing Leaders for Developing Nations, In Feldman, H. Educating for Leadership

Coming soon...

Wellness Hacks (2020) with Jamie McClean

Global Nursing...Across Generations (Working title, 2020)

Every Negotiation has Results...Are you ready for the consequences (2020)

Twelve Weeks to Service Excellence (Working title, 2020)

Every Outcome Needs a WOW (2020)

Are You Ready to Recharge Your Battery?

Made in the USA
Columbia, SC
06 May 2020

95420033R00059